FRONTLINE MINISTRIES PRESENTS

THE

GIFT

A 30-Day Devotional for Male Athletes

Matt Malone

The Gift

Published by
Frontline Ministries
www.https://gofrontline.org

Library of Congress Control Number: 2025923888

Paperback ISBN: 978-1-956033-20-5
Ebook ISBN: 978-1-956033-21-2

Printed in the United States of America

To my Savior, without YOU there is no ME.

To Punky, thank you for being my rock and consistent voice of truth and reason to keep me grounded.

To my three sons, I'm proud and humbled to be your earthly father. Now get to work on those chores.

Contents

Introduction

Have you ever heard the expression "you never know until you try"? That's the way I feel about this devotional. I've never considered myself to be a writer, or someone who successfully puts thoughts down on paper in a synchronized order that make sense. Give me a microphone and a crowd of people, and I'm good. But a pen and paper? Not so confident. However, I've learned through this process that you never know what God can do through you until you try it. Until you get uncomfortable, take a risk, and jump out of the boat to walk on water like Peter did toward Jesus.

One of my mentors from a far, Pastor Craig Groeschel, says that every leader needs to push themselves into discomfort, because one of two things will happen: either they will gain confidence or humility, and both are needed for success. I love that teaching. For you, the athlete, this may be your "jump out the boat" moment. Reading a daily devotional for thirty days may be something you've never done before. Exploring your faith in God may be foreign to you, but that's okay. I believe you are reading this introduction for a reason, and I believe you are seeking God for a reason. Embrace this moment. Take hold of this opportunity and ask God to speak to you in a very real and personal way that you have no doubt He really exists. Use this devotional like a pair of electrical cables that jump start the battery in your car. Let this journey be a jump start into your pursuit and search of God in your life. Use the space provided after each day to reflect, write down thoughts, answer questions, and work on your faith game. My hope for you is that after thirty days you will be propelled to open the Bible and begin exploring God's holy Word. His holy Word to YOU, His chosen Son. Be blessed my guy. Your journey begins now.

Sincerely,
Coach Matt

Day 1: Vision

THE WORD

"The Lord answered me: "Write down the vision; write it clearly on clay tablets so whoever reads it can run to tell others. It is not yet time for the message to come true, but that time is coming soon; the message will come true. It may seem like a long time, but be patient and wait for it, because it will surely come; it will not be delayed."

— Habakkuk 2:2–3 NCV

THE MESSAGE

I'm a goal setter. I truly believe in the power of writing down your visions and dreams. There is something divine about it. When I write down something that's important to me, something that I want really bad, I find I'm more focused and determined to accomplish it. Like in 2024 when I wrote ten goals down for the year. One of those was to meet Eddie George and get involved with his football program at Tennessee State University. He's an NFL legend who played for the Tennessee Titans.

I counted eight different people who tried to connect me into Eddie, but nothing was working.

My vision became a reality on August 23, 2024, when I attended a "meet the seniors" event on campus at TSU. I had received an email about the event and decided to take a leap and attend. As the event was winding down, I saw Eddie on the field and decided that if I was ever going to take a shot now was the time. I'm ashamed to admit this, but I was nervous like I was about to ask a girl out for the first time. I walked up, tapped his shoulder, and he turned around. I introduced myself and told him that he should put his name on the ballot for President of the United States because that's how hard it was to track him down. He laughed, the ice was broke, and then I proceeded to ask if I could help serve the team in some way as their chaplain. He told me they already had a chaplain, but he really liked my spirit and wanted me to come talk to the guys one night at chapel. He gave me his number and BOOM! Just like that I was attending their chapels for home games and visiting practice.

That story might not mean a lot to you, but it does me. Because it was my vision. It was what I wanted, what I felt the Lord had put on my heart, and to see it become a reality was incredibly rewarding. Sometimes you have to see it before anyone else will see it, and sometimes you have to believe it before anyone else will believe it. I had to put action to my faith and consistently pursue what I wanted. No one can tell me what I want. That is between me and God. The same with you. No one can tell you what your dream or vision is for your future. You must decide that and take control of your life. You only get one.

THE RESPONSE

Goals give your life focus, if you don't have any vision for your future then you're allowing life to dictate where you land. What goals do you have written down right now?

If you don't have any goals, write down five on the lines provided below. Begin to identify things that you would like to accomplish. Review your goals at least once a week to remind you of your destiny. Be SPECIFIC!

Write down goals you can measure. Vague goals equal vague results. You need to write goals that you can see if you attained or not. For example: "I want to become a better football player" is too vague. You can't measure that. Instead write something like "I want to average 7 solo tackles, 3 QB pressures, and 1 sack a game for the season." That's a goal you can measure to see if you hit or not.

Goals are meant to drive you, not deflate you. Don't get discouraged if you don't hit your goal. Be encouraged that you probably accomplished more having a goal than you would have with no goal. Write it down!

WRITE IT

REVIEW IT

BELIEVE IT

UNTIL YOU ACCOMPLISH IT

_____

_____

_____

_____

_____

_____

_____

Day 2: Plan

THE WORD

> *"People may make plans in their minds, but the Lord decides what they*
> *will do."*
>
> — Proverbs 16:9 NCV

THE MESSAGE

I distinctly remember in seventh grade writing a paper about what profession I wanted to pursue as an adult. I chose professional baseball. I just knew I was destined to be playing on the biggest stage. Despite Mrs. Lemons (yes, that was her name) trying to get me to think outside of my narrow mindedness and at least consider another profession, I was dead set on playing in the big leagues. Then I got to high school. I quickly began to realize that maybe I should alter my dream a little.

Sometimes our plan and God's plan look completely different. When I was in seventh grade I never could have imagined doing what I do now for a living. I'm an entrepreneur. I can barely spell *entrepreneur*. If it wasn't for my smart phone, I wouldn't even know what it means. My wife and I started our nonprofit organization in order to mentor, disciple, and invest into the next generation of athletes. God knew all along that I would be doing what I'm doing now, but I didn't. That's where trust comes in.

You can't see what God sees, nor do you understand what He knows, but if you let Him, He will lead and guide you to exactly where you need to be. The same God that knew you before you were in your mother's womb knows what will bring you the most satisfaction, joy, and fulfillment in life. He knows because He's the one who put that in you. Trust Him. Surrender your hopes, dreams, wishes, and desires to Him. Seek Him first above anything and everything else, and then watch as the Lord unfolds His magnificent plan for your life right before your eyes.

THE RESPONSE

When you look into the future what do you see? Where do you see your-self? What will you be doing?_____

_____

If God told you He had a better plan for your life than what you have would you trust Him?_____

_____

_____

_____

Write a prayer to God in your own words expressing any fear or anxiety about your future. Surrender your life over to Him in this prayer. Share with the Lord your deepest desires, hopes, and dreams and don't think for a second that just because He already knows them that He doesn't want to hear them from you. As you do this exercise, I pray you will feel the peace of the Lord rest on you. He's in control. Trust Him and allow Him to direct your steps, and you won't be disappointed._____

_____

_____

_____

_____

Day 3: Process

"We must not become tired of doing good. We will receive our harvest of eternal life at the right time if we do not give up."

— Galatians 6:9 NCV

THE MESSAGE

There is a process to everything in life. From the way food is grown to how a baby is formed inside a mother's womb, everything requires a process to progress to the next level. I define *process* as the steps taken to grow intentionally in whatever you want to achieve. The challenge is committing to the process. We live in a fast-paced, quick-to-rise culture where one video posted online can blow you up and gain you national or even global attention. Because of this reality, we falsely assume that we can skip the process of growth and move right to the spotlight. The problem with that is oftentimes a person's character is not developed enough to handle such stardom and success, so they burn out quickly. The process is EVERYTHING. As I get older, I'm beginning to realize how important the process is.

When I was twenty-six years old, I was the student pastor at a church. I'd been there a year, and was getting really good feedback from everyone, including my boss, my pastor. We were a mid-size suburban church outside Nashville, Tennessee, and people were moving in like crazy. After my pastor gave me a few opportunities to preach, I started to get the big dawg syndrome. All the compliments and praise on my communication abilities began to puff me up, and before long I thought that I could run the church. I didn't have a lot of respect for my pastor because I had become prideful and consumed with myself. I was blind to it, and the Lord had to take me through a yearlong process to humble me and help me see my prideful arrogance. He put me in my place to the point where I was just grateful to have a job and to serve my Savior at the same time. *Process.*

The distance between where you want to be and where you are is in the process. You should embrace what God is doing in you right now as you read these words. He's working in you, teaching you, training you, developing your character so that He can promote you and expand your territory when His timing is right. Don't skip the process.

THE RESPONSE

What is God teaching you right now about yourself?_____

_____

_____

_____

Where do you need to grow as a man and an athlete?_____

_____

_____

_____

A great question for your coach, pastor, teacher, parent, or guardian: *What character flaw do you see in me that I can't see for myself?* If you are humble enough to ask this question and receive the answer, you're going to go farther faster than your peers. Don't stop doing what is right, for at the proper time the Lord will honor you as you work the *process*.

Day 4: Consistency

"Jesus Christ is the same yesterday, today, and forever."

— Hebrews 13:8 NCV

THE MESSAGE

Talk about the epitome of consistency. Our Word for the day states that Jesus never changes. Ever. He never has an off day, one of those days that you just can't seem to find your superpower. I tend to experience those often. Over the years I've really tried hard to maintain a consistent outlook and approach to life. After all, the athletes who are able to perform at high levels for a long time are those who can maintain consistent habits every single day. Just for reference, in 2024 I set a goal to go 365 days without cheating on my diet. That's right! No cookies, no cake, no Popeyes, no pizza, no mac and cheese, no chips, no life essentially. You may be asking, Why take on such a task? For me the answer was simple: in order to get to another level, I had to push myself to do something I'd never done before. In other words, I had to up my consistency game. I slipped up on Valentine's Day and had to restart the count, but as I write today, I'm on day 368.

What are you willing to do for an entire year? Every morning for the past 537 days I've opened my Bible app to read the verse of the day. Why? Because I know I need Gods Word in my mind and heart in order for me to be the man God has called me to be. *Consistency.*

Your habits will determine your destiny. The things you do or don't do every day will either drive you to greatness or push you to mediocrity. Consistency brings safety and security. I can trust that God has my back because He never changes. Regardless of my own feelings or struggles, I can rely on the truth that Jesus is the same yesterday, today, and forever, which means I can trust His Word.

THE RESPONSE

Where do you need more consistency in your life?_____

_____

What are you willing to do every day for 365 days?_____

_____

_____

Day 5: Struggle

The Word

"Let everyone be subject to the governing authorities, for there is no au-
thority except that which God has established. The authorities that exist
have been established by God."

— Romans 13:1 NIV

The Message

Do you struggle with authority? Do you have a hard time submitting to a coach, teacher, police officer, parent, or anyone else in an authoritative role? I hate to admit it, but this is one I've had to wrestle with throughout the years. We all have blind spots. Blind spots are areas in our life that we literally can't see because we are "blind" to them. Oftentimes we need God to open our eyes to help us see what we can't see for ourselves.

My struggle with authority began when I started college. In my eyes, I had submitted to God, the ultimate authority, and therefore I didn't need anyone else telling me what to do or how to do it. As I got older, I began to "do me," and disregard my parents, professors, and bosses at work. I was self-righteously confident that because I was walking with God no one could tell me how to live my life. Looking back, it was a dangerous mindset.

The issue continued as I stepped into my first "real job" working as a youth pastor at a church outside of Nashville. After a year at the church, I began to get confident in my calling and my skill set so much so that I sort of thought that I could be the senior pastor. As I mentioned in Day 3's message, I began to lose respect for my pastor, who was my boss, and didn't give much regard to his input. It was a heart and pride issue. I was twenty-five years old at the time and thought I knew everything I needed to know to be the top guy. Until God humbled me.

God didn't use just one event or moment to humble me. Instead, it was a series of events that took place roughly over an entire year when God had to really get my attention. My behavior and my pride were catching up to me, and the Lord had to sit me down or else I was heading toward self-destruction. I was hardheaded and didn't want to listen. I wanted to make up my own rules. The problem with that mentality was that it was rooted in pride, and the Bible is clear that pride always comes before destruction.

Through many tough and uncomfortable conversations with my pastor, the Lord began to reveal the root cause behind my lack of respect for authority. There is always a root, and for me it was the fact that I couldn't trust my parents growing up. My biological father died from alcohol abuse when I was four. When I began high school, my mom was not in a good place, and my stepdad, although he was a phenomenal provider, didn't connect with me much on a personal level. So the very people in my life that I should be trusting to lead and guide me weren't my guides at all. Jesus was.

By God's grace, I submitted my life to the Lord when I as twelve years old, and in my mind, because I was trusting God to guide me through His Word, the Bible, I developed a sense of independence. I didn't think I needed anyone in authority telling me what to do. I didn't realize it at the time, but God was revealing my pride to me like opening a book for the first time. The Lord literally had to break me down in order to build me back up, and I'm so incredibly grateful He did.

What the Lord taught me was that when we surrender and respect the authority that He puts in place for us, we experience the Lord's goodness and blessing. When we buck the system, however, we experience brokenness and hardship. It was a valuable lesson that I try and hold close to me to this day, and I hope you learn it much quicker than I did.

THE RESPONSE

Do you struggle with authority in your own life? If so, who do you struggle with specifically? Why?_____

_____

_____

_____

Who is someone in authority over you that you respect and admire?
Why?_____

_____

_____

_____

Respecting authority begins with surrendering to Gods authority and
trusting that He knows what's best for you. As you begin to respect those
in authority whether they deserve it or not, God will bless you because
you're being obedient to Romans 13:1.

Day 6: Pain

THE WORD

"In all things God works for the good of those who love Him, who have been called according to His purpose."

— Romans 8:28 NIV

THE MESSAGE

Today's verse of the day is one that God has used to get me through some dark days. In yesterday's devotional I talked about the struggle that we sometimes face with other people. I shared about my struggle with authority and how the Lord had to shift my mindset during that time of struggle. Today, I want to dive a little deeper into one of the most painful moments I have experienced in my life.

I never thought I would get a divorce. As a pastor, I even low-key judged people who were divorced. Having worked as a student pastor, I had seen the effects divorce can have on kids and I just knew I wouldn't put my two sons through that mess—until we did.

Chances are you have experienced the sting of divorce in your life or in the life of someone close to you. Unfortunately, it's way too common nowadays. In fact, not too long ago I was taking a young man home from a college visit. He was a rising senior in high school with crazy athletic talent but had been expelled from school for being in the wrong place at the wrong time with the wrong crowd. I began to dig and ask my guy questions about his childhood. It turns out, his father was in prison, and his stepdaddy and mother divorced when he was in eighth grade. It had crushed this young man. Divorce is hard on adults, but it's even harder on the children.

Divorce is not God's plan, and now I know why. Divorce divides and separates. It causes friction and tension within the family unit while bringing chaos into the world of the child. My divorce was one of the most challenging and painful experiences I've ever endured, not just because of my own emotional health, but over concern for my two sons and how they would respond. That's why today's verse of the day played such a crucial role in helping me get through those dark and lonely days.

God's word never returns void. In other words, it never fails. The Lord taught me a very valuable truth while walking through my valley moment: GOD DON'T WASTE PAIN. Instead, He recycles it and uses it for good, not only for the one enduring it but also for ones in the future who will endure something similar. What you must understand about any painful experience in life is that you're not just enduring it for yourself but for someone else later down the road. For someone that you've never met yet. For someone that is going to need your testimony of how you came through by God's grace.

We never go through pain for nothing. Jesus didn't endure the pain of the cross for nothing. He did it to rescue this fallen world from sin. There is purpose in pain. Hallelujah to that truth. Be encouraged today. Your parents may be going through a divorce right now, or someone you know may be experiencing that pain, but take heart. For the Lord is in the midst of your struggle, walking with you through the pain, and ultimately preparing you for a powerful testimony that will help someone in the future.

I thank God for those days in my life because without them I wouldn't be the man that I am today. It was in the lonely days spent in the basement of a house that wasn't mine in the middle of March 2020, when we were all quarantined and I was barely getting to see my sons, that the Lord began to reshape me and change me from the inside out. Sometimes it's in our moments of darkness when the Lord speaks the loudest, not because that's when He likes to speak, but because that's when we are more open to listen. It was in that basement that I was desperate to hear from Him. I'm not sure what you're going through right now as you read this, but one thing I know for sure: GOD DON'T WASTE PAIN, and He isn't wasting yours. Surrender and submit your life and your situation to Him and watch Him move.

THE RESPONSE

What's the most challenging thing you've faced in life thus far?_____

What's the most challenging thing you're facing right now?

_____

_____

What is God teaching you through your pain?_____

_____

_____

Has your view of pain and suffering changed after reading this devotional? _____

How has God used your pain from the past to help someone else?

_____

_____

Day 7: Resilience

THE WORD

"For though the righteous fall seven times, they rise again, but the wicked stumble when calamity strikes."

— Proverbs 24:16 NIV

THE MESSAGE

Have you ever made a mistake during a game? Of course you have if you're human. I just watched the kicker for the University of Tennessee miss a game ending field goal to beat the University of Georgia for the first time in nine years this past weekend. Imagine how he felt? Over one hundred thousand people are watching you, depending on you, rooting for you, and you miss. How does he bounce back? How will he respond?

We all fall short at some point. Last summer I was asked to speak for a Little League baseball team as they were trying to make it to the Little League World Series. I've been speaking long enough to know whether or not I made a connection, and by God's grace that day I slammed one across the fence. It was a powerful moment, and the coach asked me to come back and talk to the guys before their championship game. I went in confident that I could inspire them to victory, but for some reason that day those twelve-year-olds and I didn't quite connect like a few days before. Baseball isn't like football, and my pregame hype speech fell flat. It was terrible. They ended up losing by one run, but thankfully they had another game the next night since they were in the winner's bracket of a double elimination tournament.

I couldn't sleep that night. I wore that loss as if I was the kicker for UT. That's how serious I take my craft. I was determined to bounce back, so I decided to show up early the next night to redeem myself. I was prayed up and ready to go. I stepped onto the field, but before I could even get past the dugout, one of the assistant coaches stopped me. I'll never forget what he said, "we don't need your motivation tonight, bud. The guys can motivate themselves."

Wow! That hurt. I've been blessed to speak in front of college, high school, and middle school athletes, but to have an assistant coach of a twelve-year-old's baseball team say those words was humbling. I felt like an ant. I wanted to dig a hole and literally bury myself in hiding from my embarrassment. To make matters worse, my twelve-year-old son came up to me as I walked off the field and asked me why I wasn't speaking. He went to school with a handful of guys on the team, which put an exclamation mark on a rough night at the office. I was crushed. I couldn't even watch the game. I just remember taking a walk as far as I could go so that I couldn't hear the PA announcer. *Resilience.*

Resilience is the ability to bounce back and push through adversity. It's getting back up when you get knocked down, and that day I felt like

Muhammad Ali took a cut at me. But you know what? I'm still here by God's grace, and I'm still speaking and inspiring athletes to maximize their God-given potential on and off the field. I had to take my pain and hurt to God for the next few weeks. I journaled my experience. I even created an acronym to deal with it.

P - process it

A - admit it

I - illuminate it

N - name it

This acronym helped me process through my emotions. When you fail and make mistakes, when you feel that you blew your shot and may never get another one, when you feel hopeless and lonely, just know you are not alone. If you admit your pain and give it to the Lord, He will turn your mess into a powerful message to share with others. Just like I'm doing now with you. Remember, God don't waste pain. And He won't waste yours. So get back up. Hit the gym. Train. Do something hard today, and remind yourself that your mistakes don't define you, they create you into an indestructible force. You will RISE again. Let's get it!

THE RESPONSE

Think of a time when you failed in athletics or life. How did it feel?

_____

_____

How did you handle it?_____

_____

Are you satisfied with how you've responded?_____

How can you respond differently in the future when you get knocked down again?_____

_____

_____

What is God teaching you in the midst of your failure?_____

_____

_____

Day 8: Persistence

"We must not become tired of doing good. We will receive our harvest of eternal life at the right time if we do not give up."
— Galatians 6:9 NCV

THE MESSAGE

I love warm weather, especially in spring and summer. Being outside, taking walks with the fam, beating my wife in pickle ball—I just love it. The one thing I don't like about summer, however, are bugs—gnats in particular. They're always trying to ruin a good outing when you're enjoying food with the people that you love. You kill one, but they just keep multiplying. It's crazy.

If I can say anything positive about one of God's creations, it's that they are *persistent*. They just keep coming at you regardless of how you feel about them. They continue to show up and mess with your good time.

As athletes we must take on that level of persistence when it comes to the way we attack sports and life. You will face rejection. Not everyone will like you or sing your praises. Some will be jealous of your ability and throw shade because they aren't like you. They secretly envy what you bring to the table and who you are. You won't get along with every coach you play for. Some coaches will have their favorites, and unfortunately you won't be that guy.

When I started Frontline Ministries, I was looking to get involved at the university level. I had a specific university in mind but zero connections into the athletic department. After trying a few leads and getting nowhere, I decided to just show up. I put on my best three-piece suit and drove down to campus. I remember feeling nervous but praying that the Lord would go before me and grant me favor. The goal was to meet with the men's basketball coach. Looking back, I was really naive, but you don't know what you don't know, so I was putting faith in action. I made my way to the gymnasium and wondered into the girls' basketball department where the coaches' offices were located. I was sharply dressed which gave off the "I mean business" vibe, so when I asked to meet with the head coach of the men's team, one of the assistants took me to his office. As I waited, I was confident. Rehearsing my lines over and over in my head, making my appeal to be the chaplain of their team.

Then it happened. The double doors flung open and here came the head coach walking down the hall. I stood up and immediately felt my stomach drop. It was probably one of the most awkward first meetings I can remember. The coach dropped the pen he was carrying to shake my hand, and we almost bumped heads trying to pick it up. Unbelievable. I shook his hand; he invited me into his office and told me he had five minutes. I could already feel the tension. For the next three minutes I struggled to regurgitate everything I had rehearsed. I felt like a salesman trying to sell a car to a bird. It wasn't happening. The coach was gracious, asked if I had a card, and then sent me on my way. Talk about humbling.

At that point I had a choice to make. Give up or fly back. I hate losing, and that day I felt like a big fat *L*. I went to my corner, regrouped, and a few months later went back down to campus. Except this time I had a partner, someone who actually graduated from the university and who could sell bark to a tree. He also happened to be the chairman of our nonprofit. As he took my wife and I around campus, we ran into the basketball coaches walking to the cafeteria. I immediately got nervous, thinking he would remember me and our awkward exchange. This time, though, was different. Mainly because someone else was there to endorse me and my work instead of me trying to sell myself. The connection was made, and I began to visit the team a few weeks later.

Persistence.

THE RESPONSE

Have you ever got rejected? How did you feel? How did you respond?

_____

_____

What drives you to keep pushing despite initial challenge or adversity?

_____

_____

If at first you don't succeed, try again, and again, and again. It's been said that Thomas Edison failed thousands of times trying to get the light bulb to work. "I have not failed, I've just found 10,000 ways that won't work," he is credited with saying. This is so powerful for you and me. We must continue to show up for what we want. Sometimes it's not the most talented who get the position, but the most persistent. Go get it today!

Day 9: Fear

The Word

*"The fear of the LORD is the beginning of wisdom, and knowledge of the
Holy One is understanding."*

— Proverbs 9:10 NIV

The Message

There are two types of fear in life. Fear that paralyzes you and fear
that pushes you. I appreciate where I came from. I'm extremely grateful
for my family and the circumstances I experienced as a child because they
helped shape who I am today. However, I don't want to go back. Memories
flood my mind of my mom being choked against the wall by her boyfriend
and her telling me, a seven-year-old, to call 911. I have a fear of going
back to the place I was born. I don't want to take my wife and three sons
back there to live. That fear drives me. It pushes me, motivates me, keeps
me focused through challenging and difficult seasons because I don't want
to move back home.

Not all fear is bad. The fear of the Lord is the beginning of wisdom the Bible tells us (Proverbs 9:10). When we have a proper fear of God and His commandments, we are motivated to serve Him and follow His Word. If we don't fear God and His judgment, then we live however we want to live. If a child has no authority in their home, they are left to live a life without boundaries, which can ultimately lead to their destruction. I see this regularly in the young men that I work with. Without a father in the home, oftentimes teenage boys begin to drift. Without structure they tend to wander into trouble and lose focus on what really matters in life. Every child needs a loving authority figure to help set rules and expectations around their life to follow. Children thrive in those environments because they are safe and secure. We are no different.

The Response

What are you afraid of from your past?_____

_____

What "fears" drive you and keeps you motivated toward success?

_____

_____

What are you afraid of that paralyzes you from taking the next step or making the next move?

_____

_____

Who's your authority figure? Who do you trust to offer loving advice and discipline when needed?_____

_____

_____

Day 10: Breakthrough

"With God's power working in us, God can do much, much more than anything we can ask or imagine."

— Ephesians 3:20 NCV

THE MESSAGE

Have you ever hit your stride as a player? Have you ever felt like all the work and training you've been putting in is paying off? It's a powerful thing. My wife and I are four years deep into starting our own ministry. It's scary starting your own business because if it fails there is no one to blame or point fingers at except yourself. The rewards, however, are worth it. The freedom that we have to minister to who we want and how we want was the vision God gave me back in 2020 during Covid. I was working for a large organization at the time but was having difficulty finding freedom within the organization because of the structure and boundaries that were in place. I understood it. When you are a world-wide nonprofit you must have rules and laws in place to facilitate order, but for me it was hindering my growth and killing my passion.

Most things in life will cost you. Jesus said if you want to build a tower, you must first sit down and count the cost (Luke 14:28). Otherwise, you may begin building and then run out of money. Likewise, chasing your dream will cost you. It has me. You might not be able to attend all the parties, be at the social gatherings, drink alcohol, smoke weed, pop pills, sleep around, or do the things that your peers are doing. You may feel like the only one sometimes, and the road may be lonely, but stay faithful. Your breakthrough is coming, and it will be fully satisfying and rewarding when you can sit back and watch as the Lord does immeasurably more than you could even think or imagine. I can't believe the Lord has brought us this far in our ministry. I can't believe that I'm actually writing this devotional. I never dreamed I would ever be writing anything! I'm from New Market, Tennessee! College wasn't talked about in my family. No one ever went to college in my family, so it wasn't even a thought. But God . . .

The number of lives that have been touched through Frontline Ministries over the years is humbling. The scholarships, the Bibles, the meals, the words of truth that we've been blessed to give over these past four years is incredible. All because by God's grace we took a leap of faith and decided to trust the Lord at His Word. Don't get me wrong, we definitely aren't where we want to be, but thank God we're not where we used to be either.

Your breakthrough is coming, young blood. Stay consistent, count the cost of what you must give up, and chase that dream that God has put in you with everything you have.

THE RESPONSE

What is your dream?_____

_____

What are you willing to give up to chase it?_____

_____

How will you separate yourself from your peers?_____

_____

Imagine what your "breakthrough" will look like when you make it to the other side.

_____

_____

Day 11: Curveballs

"The LORD is close to the brokenhearted, and he saves those whose spirits have been crushed."

— Psalms 34:18 NCV

THE MESSAGE

On May 7, 2022, the unexpected happened. My friend Kip Yount was pronounced dead at Vanderbilt Hospital as a result of a lung that collapsed during the night. Kip was a fighter. He had spent several weeks at Vandy. They called him the sickest patient in the hospital. Unfortunately, the circumstances that led to his death were not his fault. He had had his gall bladder removed at another hospital a few weeks prior. It's a very common surgery in our country and was expected to be in and out. At least that was the plan.

I'll never forget being at the gym when I received a phone call from Kip's mother Ms. Polli. I could hear the desperation in her voice as she proceeded to tell me that Kip wasn't doing well and asked if I could come pray with them at the hospital. I immediately took off. My mind was racing. As I walked into the waiting room and felt the heaviness of the situation, I began to learn the details of why Kip was struggling. The doctor accidentally cut Kips liver while removing the gall bladder and didn't realize it. They proceeded to sew him up thinking he was ok, but had no idea he was bleeding internally from the incision. To complicate matters, the doctor had left the next day to go on vacation, so there was no one capable of operating on Kip at the hospital. It was a desperate scene. They had to get Kip stable enough to air lift him to Vanderbilt, one of the most prestigious hospitals in the country. Once there, the doctors told us they didn't expect him to make it through the night, but they didn't know Kip. Not only did he make it through the night, he made it through several nights before his body gave out.

Life is hard sometimes. Life doesn't care what your last name is, how much money you have in your account, or where you come from. Life will sucker punch you. That's what Kips death felt like. It was as if someone snuck up behind us and pulled the rug out from underneath our feet, leaving us lying helplessly on the ground, trying to make sense of what just happened.

You will face curveballs in life. You will have to deal with pain and tragedy at some point. Unfortunately, it's part of the fallen, jacked-up, messed-up world we live in. Take heart, however, because we serve a God who understands pain. Jesus never deserved to be crucified. He was innocent. He did nothing wrong, but he was treated like a criminal and given the most excruciating form of punishment in those days. We serve a God who can relate to the curveballs in our lives.

It's been almost three years since Kip's passing, and we have created an award in his name that we give each year at our fundraising banquet to honor a young athlete who has handled tremendous adversity, just like Kip did. Along with the award comes a scholarship for them to pursue their God-given dream and vision for their life. We can't bring Kip back, but we can learn how to hit curveballs, and by God's grace that's what we've done. Turned a negative into a positive that remembers Kip's legacy and blesses the next generation. That's where healing truly begins. By first acknowledging, accepting, and embracing your pain, then using that pain to help someone else. Jesus endured the cross, but after three days of lying in the grave, He got up. With His help, we can get up too.

THE RESPONSE

What's the most difficult thing you've ever experienced in life?_____

_____

How did you handle it?_____

_____

_____

How have you been able to somehow turn the negative into a positive to benefit others?_____

_____

_____

What's the first step you need to take in healing from a past hurt?_____

_____

_____

Day 12: Reality

"The LORD says, "My thoughts are not like your thoughts. Your ways are not like my ways. Just as the heavens are higher than the earth, so are my ways higher than your ways and my thoughts higher than your thoughts."
— Isaiah 55:8–9 NCV

The Message

Accepting reality is hard. Just ask Nate Graham. I met Nate a few years ago, but really have gotten to know him this past year. Nate is a wrester and to say he is an inspiration is an understatement.

In eighth grade, Nate was diagnosed with scoliosis. Over the years tension had built up in his spine as a result of the pressure he was putting on his body, and blood began to slip into his spinal cord. One day as Nate was coming home from a summer camp in Michigan, he realized he couldn't move his arms or legs. He had just woken up from a nap and went to move to another seat but couldn't. He thought he would lie there for a few minutes and try again, but still no feeling or movement. That's when reality set in. Nate was *paralyzed*.

After his teammates informed the coach of the situation, they pulled the bus over and called the nearest paramedics. They had to carry Nate off the bus to get him on the stretcher to take him to the hospital. Can you imagine? You're fifteen years old, been physically active your entire life, and suddenly you can't move? Unbelievable. Imagine what was going through Nate's head. Would he ever wrestle again? Forget wrestling. Would he ever be able to walk again or feed himself?! Talk about a reality check. Wow.

They did an MRI as soon as Nate got to the hospital and found bleeding in his spine, which was causing the temporary paralysis. Thank God the doctors were able to remove the blood. After three days of being paralyzed, Nate began to receive feeling in his arms and legs again. After almost nine months of no training whatsoever, Nate stepped onto the wrestling mat for his first match since he was paralyzed. He won. And he kept on winning. He now has over one hundred wins in his high school career and just became the first state champion in his school's history with an overtime take down in the finals match at the state championships. It's an unreal story for an unreal kid who serves an unreal God.

I'm not sure what you're facing right now in your life, but this I know for sure: God has a plan. We may not understand His plan in the moment, but if we can trust that even through the pain God is working it out for our good. Then we can boldly face whatever scenario life wants to throw at us. Remember: God's thoughts are not ours, and His ways are so much more advanced. He sees what we can't, and He knows what we don't. Trust Him. He's got you.

THE RESPONSE

What's your current reality that you need to accept?_____

_____

_____

What is most difficult about accepting this reality that you're in?_____

_____

_____

Do you believe that God is for you and not against you? Do you believe
that He is working your reality out for your good?_____

_____

Be encouraged today. Your breakthrough is coming. Just hold on one
day longer and watch what God will do.

Day 13: Identity

THE WORD

"Therefore, if anyone is in Christ, he is a new creation; old things have passed away; behold, all things have become new."

— 2 Corinthians 5:17 NKJV

THE MESSAGE

One of the most important questions you must answer as a man is this: Who Am I? Oftentimes I tell my athletes to look themselves in the mirror and ask this question. There's something powerful about looking deep into your own eyes and reflecting on who you are as a man. Once you've established your identity, then you can start building upon your foundation. If you don't have a strong sense of who you are, then it will be hard to lead other men. When temptation comes, it is easier to give in if you don't have a firm identity. When trials and hard times pop up in life, you will struggle to conquer them if your identity is not established and rooted in Christ your Savior. Identity is key to unlocking the door to your greatest potential as a man and an athlete.

The first step in establishing your identity is to understand who created you and why you were created. The Bible says that before you were even in your mother's womb, God knew you. Wow! That's a crazy thought. Before your momma knew you, God already had you in His mind. He knows how many hairs are on your head. He knows every detail about you because He is the one who created you. He knows what will bring you fulfillment and satisfaction. He knows your hopes, dreams, wishes, and deepest desires, and more importantly, He knows what you need.

When you begin to seek the Lord and surrender to His authority, you will begin to find yourself. The man that God created you to be. A strong, confident, secure, stable, humble, mighty, and fierce man of God that will be a force in this life on earth. Before you can find that part of you, however, you must surrender and allow the Lord to kill the old you that is filled with lust and pride so that He can create the new you filled with His Spirit and life. The old has gone; behold the new has come. This spiritual process that happens on the inside of a man begins with surrender, and as men that's not easy for us to do. We are prideful by nature and stubborn. We want to handle our business, and we don't like to lean on someone else for help. Our Creator is the only one who can truly change us from the inside out. We *need* Him. Without Him we are a mess. In order for us to discover our destiny in life and experience ultimate satisfaction, we must first give up our life to the one who gave up His on the cross. Once we do that, we will begin to find ourselves and who God made us to be. Then, we can't be stopped.

THE RESPONSE

Have you ever surrendered your life to Christ? Have you ever given up and told the Lord that you no longer want to live for yourself or this world, but for Him? If so, describe that day and moment. What did you feel after surrendering?_____

_____

_____

_____

Who are you? Write down three words that describe who you are as a man. They are "I Am" statements. Example: I am bold. I am intelligent. I am confident. _____

_____

_____

You will always need to remind yourself of who you are when you start to doubt or feel insecure as a man. Trust me, it will happen. I have a list of "I Am" statements that I go back to whenever I need a reminder of who I am and who God has called me to be. I repeat them until I believe them. You should too.

Day 14: Passion

"Whatever you do, work at it with all your heart, as working for the Lord, not for human masters,"

— Colossians 3:23 NIV

THE MESSAGE

Passion is everything. You can have two people performing the same job, one with passion and the other with obligation. One wants to be there and work, while the other wants to be somewhere else and is just passing the time. We all know the difference. Have you ever played for a coach that's not invested? The key ingredient they lack is the most essential of them all: passion. Passion is the difference between great teams and decent ones. Passion inspires us to be excellent in whatever we are trying to accomplish in life. I love what I do for a living because I'm blessed to live my passion for helping young athletes grow in their relationship with Christ while also reaching new levels athletically.

It was the Lord's passion for His sheep that drove Him to the cross to be crucified. Jesus didn't want to be crucified. Who would? Getting stripped naked, spit on, beaten, having a crown of thorns pressed against your skull, receiving forty lashes with a whip that has sharp pieces of bone tied at the end of it, then having to carry your own eighty-pound crossbeam up a hill, having nine-inch nails driven through your hands and feet, and finally being left there to hang and die while in excruciating pain. Who in their right mind would want that?

Passion. Jesus did what He did because of *you*. It was for you and me that Christ died to set us free from the bondage of sin. Without His sacrifice we would have no hope of living with Him in eternity one day. That kind of love and sacrifice you won't find in a female, a sport, a hobby, or other interest. That kind of passion is only found in God. Today, if you are struggling to find the motivation to continue on with practice or finishing your season, I pray that Christ's death on the cross is a reminder for you that God really does care about you and the details of your life. You are not alone. You can trust Him with your frustration, pain, disappointment, and failures. It knows how to recharge your batteries and bring life to your mediocrity. Jesus is the *passion* you are looking for. Trust Him.

THE RESPONSE

Where are you lacking passion in your life right now?_____

_____

_____

What area are you settling for mediocrity and not giving your all?_____

_____

_____

How does the example of Jesus' death inspire you?_____

_____

_____

Remember: you only get one life. One shot. One opportunity to live on this planet. What will you do with it today?

Day 15: Lessons

THE WORD

"The Lord disciplines those he loves, and he punishes everyone he accepts as his child.""

— Hebrews 12:6 NCV

THE MESSAGE

Being disciplined is never fun. Especially when you are on the receiving end. A few years back I had a crack on my windshield. It was one of those cracks that began as a small dot, but over the course of time it grew like a mountain range in Colorado. I knew eventually I had to get it replaced, but I didn't want to spend the money to do it. My uncle told me I could file a claim with my insurance, and they would cover the cost. So I did. While filing the claim, the insurance agent asked me how the crack happened. I honestly didn't remember, but I did know what made it worse. My windshield was frozen with ice during the last winter storm we had, and I did the very thing they tell you not to do. I poured

56

hot water on my windshield to thaw the ice. This can actually crack your windshield. Instead of telling the insurance agent the truth, I lied and said that a rock hit the windshield while driving down the interstate one day. No questions were asked, and the next week I had a new windshield for free.

The Bible is clear. You reap what you sow, and you can't cheat God. I had 295,000 miles on my car. I was focused on getting to 300,000. Up to that point I had never been in a car accident that was my fault either. All that changed about a month later. A vehicle suddenly stopped in the road, and I slammed on my brakes but rearended them anyway. That new windshield I got was useless because I totaled my car and never made it to 300,000 miles. What's worse, I had to spend over $12,000 to buy another car to drive. In essence, I traded a few hundred dollars for a new windshield for over twelve grand for another vehicle. You can't cheat God.

It occurred to me sometime after that what the Lord was trying to teach me. I was being disciplined. Does the Lord give us all that we deserve for our sins? Thankfully not. His mercy is great. However, He also disciplines those whom He loves so that we can grow and develop into the men He has called us to be. The fact was I lied, and even though I can try and justify a "little white lie," those little white lies add up to bigger lies if not kept in check. The Lord wants what's best for His children, and He can't give us His best if we aren't being honest.

Have you ever been disciplined by the Lord before? Do you know what it feels like? I wish I could tell you that discipline stops at a certain age, but that's not the truth. We aren't perfect, which means we need the Lord to correct us when we're in the wrong. He doesn't discipline us because He wants too. He disciplines us because He needs to in order for us to grow into the men that He has called us to be.

THE RESPONSE

Has the Lord ever disciplined you? What happened? How did it feel?

_____

_____

What lesson did you learn?_____

_____

_____

Day 16: The Comeback

THE WORD

"But those who wait on the LORD shall renew their strength; They shall mount up with wings like eagles, They shall run and not be weary, They shall walk and not faint."

— Isaiah 40:31 NKJV

THE MESSAGE

The Eagles won the Super Bowl in 2025. To my surprise they dominated the Kansas City Chiefs, who were attempting to be the first team in history to win three straight Super Bowls. Jalen Hurts was the quarterback, and his story inspires me. He played for one of the greatest coaches of all time, Nick Saban at the University of Alabama. During the national championship game, he got benched at halftime. Tua Tagovailoa, the backup quarterback, led Bama to a comeback win for the ages. Can you imagine how Jalen must have felt? All season he was the team's leader, but in the most crucial game of the year he played terribly and got benched in front of the whole country. Then he has to watch as his backup lead the team to a national championship, and somehow he has to be happy about it on the outside. Thats crazy to me. One would think, especially nowadays with the transfer portal, that Jalen would have transferred that next season. Instead, he stayed to finish his degree and compete for the starting job at quarterback. He didn't win the job and was subject to playing backup the entire next season. During the SEC championship game, the Crimson Tide where down against Georgia (the team that almost beat them the year before in the national championship game) when Tua went down with an injury. Guess who led the comeback? The same kid who got benched the year before against the same team! I wish I could make this up, but I can't. What a turnaround. From starter to backup to hero, and now to Super Bowl champion. Jalen ended up transferring after that season to Oklahoma, and then got drafted by the Philadelphia Eagles. Amazing story.

In life and in sports you will experience setbacks. They happen to us all, even the greatest of athletes. How you come back from those setbacks is what separates the good from the great. Jalen didn't run from adversity or hide in embarrassment. He owned his mistakes and sought to improve, and that's what led to this Super Bowl run. Nothing can stop Jalen but Jalen. He's been through the fire; he's made it through the test. He is a refined diamond that has been shaped by immense amounts of pressure, and that's why he's successful. That is why *you* will be successful as well. Don't shy away from adversity or pain. Embrace it. For it is the very tool that the Lord will use to hone, mold, and shape you into an indestructible force that can't be stopped. Wait upon the Lord during trials and injuries. Wait upon the Lord during setbacks and failures. Let the Lord strengthen you, mount you up on wings like Eagles, and then you won't become weary or tired any longer. But you will outlast your competition because of the Lord's strength in you.

THE RESPONSE

What setback are you now experiencing?_____

_____

_____

Describe a time of "failure" in your life or athletic career._____

_____

_____

What have you learned from it?_____

_____

_____

Did you embrace it or run from it?_____

_____

_____

Have you made excuses for your mistakes or owned them?_____

_____

_____

I encourage you to write Isaiah 40:31 down on a sticky note or index card and tape it to your bathroom mirror or steering wheel cover. Somewhere you can see it every day, and be reminded that God is in the process of writing *your* comeback story. Keep fightin', my guy.

Day 17: Calling

The Word

" 'Before I made you in your mother's womb, I chose you. Before you were born, I set you apart for a special work. I appointed you as a prophet to the nations.' "

— Jeremiah 1:5 NCV

The Message

The summer before my eighth grade year I was home alone watching porn. I can't even lie. I began switching the channels looking for another flick when I landed on a preacher presenting the Gospel of Jesus Christ. I couldn't change the channel. I tried. I wanted to, but I couldn't. God wouldn't let me.

By this time, my mom had remarried after my dad passed away, and financially things were as good as they ever had been up to that point in my life. Missing, however, was the influence of Granny and my Aunty B. I was blessed to have those two angels in my life as a young boy. They took me to church and taught me about the Lord, so I had enough head knowledge about Jesus but zero heart knowledge. I was quickly heading down a dangerous path trying to fulfill my souls deepest longing for love and acceptance. The hole from my father's passing was still wide open, and my attempt to fill it with pornography and baseball wasn't working. I was lost and needed guidance. My mom and stepdad are phenomenal, and I'm extremely grateful for them both, but they couldn't provide me the answers that I was looking for.

That night as I listened to the pastor preach his message, the Holy Spirit convicted me. I knew what I was doing was wrong, and I knew I wasn't living right. When the pastor gave an invitation to receive Christ, I got on my knees that night in my living room and surrendered everything to God. I told Him how sorry I was for my sins. I asked Him to forgive me and cleanse me of all my wrongs. Then I asked Him to help me live for Him for the rest of my life. It was a powerful and unforgettable moment for me. One reason is because I was always a troubled sleeper. I would often times sleepwalk in the middle of the night, but that night was different. I remember waking up the next morning having slept the entire night like a baby. For the first time in my life, I had peace. God's peace. The kind of peace that you have to experience because it's "so hard to put into words" kind of peace, and that's when my life changed.

I began to seek the Lord. I had tasted and seen that He was good, and I wanted more. As I began to search for Christ and read the Bible, I began to realize my calling. I began to understand that I was put on this earth for a purpose, and that purpose was far bigger than myself. The Lord was showing me step by step who I was. God gave me a vision for my life that I had never had before. He encouraged me with truths like the one we read today from Jeremiah, which reminds me that He has chosen me for a special work, and I am uniquely gifted and designed to accomplish everything He has called me to do.

Once I understood and felt His love and forgiveness, I began to walk differently. I had a newfound confidence not in myself but in the Creator of the universe, and the same God who called me is the same God calling you! Have you ever surrendered your life to Christ before? Have you ever had that moment in time where you came face-to-face with your sin and realized that your best option was to come to the Lord for forgiveness? If not, today is your time! Right now, wherever you are, get on your knees and cry out to God. Confess your sins, tell Him what a mess you are, and ask Him to come into your life and forgive you, cleanse you, and make you ready for service. This is your calling. Today. Right now. In Jesus' name, amen.

THE RESPONSE

Describe that moment when you gave your life to Christ. Where were you? How did you feel? What did you experience afterwards?_____

_____

_____

Oftentimes God doesn't reveal all His secrets to us at once, because we wouldn't be able to handle it. It is through a process of learning, growing, failing, and seeking day after day that the Lord reveals His plan to us. By reading this devotional today, you are taking a step toward your destiny. Don't stop!

Day 18: Rejection

The Word

"What, then, shall we say in response to these things? If God is for us, who can be against us?"

— Romans 8:31 NIV

The Message

I was a junior in college and thought I had found the one. You know, the girl that I was destined to marry. She was attractive, smart, a follower of Christ, parents had money, and she was a softball player. (I always had a thing for softball girls.) We had just began dating right before the semester ended, and her parents decided to fly me down to Orlando for a week at the beach. Orlando was her hometown, and her dad owned a flooring business. Little did I know, her parents were scouting me out to see if I was fit for their only daughter. I was clueless. The first few days were spent working with her dad. I assumed he wanted to see what kind of work ethic I had, or maybe what kind of business sense I possessed in order to one day potentially pass his company down to me. Unfortunately, I had zero experience in flooring, but I did work my butt off to show that I was a worthy companion.

As the week progressed, I could sense that I was being watched, judged, and looked down upon for some of my unorthodox actions. For example, we were eating dinner one night and had corn on the cob. I'm from New Market, Tennessee, a town of thirteen hundred people. When we eat corn on the cob, we slather that thing with butter and race to see who's the quickest to finish. They didn't do that. Instead, they used a knife and cut the corn off the cob. I thought that was interesting. As I began to tear into that corn like a caged animal who hadn't eaten in weeks, they just looked at me like I was from another planet. I was just eating like I always ate. Elbows up baby! Clear out! Make that food work! I guess they didn't see it that way.

I could sense the mood beginning to shift. I'm not the most intellectual guy, but the Lord has given me some emotional sense, and I knew something was off. On the second to last day of my trip I woke up to a letter sitting by my bed. It was from the girl. She detailed how awesome and amazing I was, how she admired my walk with God, but just didn't seem like it was the right time for us to pursue a relationship. In other words, you're not the one. I was crushed. On top of that I had to spend one more day with her family, pretending like I was okay when really I wasn't. Then I had to get on a plane and fly back to Knoxville feeling like I wasn't good enough.

Have you ever been rejected before? Maybe not by a girl, but from a college, a coach, a parent, or some other loved one? It stings not feeling good enough, but as time went on the Lord slowly began to show me how He works all things out for His good. Even when we experience rejection, it's the Lord's way of protecting us and preparing us for something better. Remember, we can't see what God sees, and if God is for us, then who can stand against us? Even if they reject you God is the one who defends you. Look at Kurt Warner. Kurt went undrafted in the 1994 NFL draft to the Green Bay Packers, only to be released before the season started. He was literally bagging groceries at a supermarket before he got an opportunity to play in the Arena Football League. Thirty-two teams rejected him, until the St. Louis Rams (now the Los Angeles Rams), took a shot and signed him. He paid them back by winning Super Bowl 34, and was named Super Bowl MVP that game.

God is your defender. He is your shelter when you get rejected. Don't run to a drug, some weed, a girl, or alcohol. Those things numb the pain temporarily and just dig a deeper pit for you to climb out of. Instead, run to Christ, your Savior. Let Him restore you, build you, and comfort you. Let Him work His plan out in you and through you for His glory. I promise it's worth it.

I didn't end up marrying that girl, and I'm thankful I didn't. That family dynamic wouldn't have worked for me. Too much helicopter parenting and overseeing. I need my space and freedom to be the man Gods called me to be. What you and I may view as rejection, the Lord sees as protection. Just know that when you experience rejection, God's really protecting you so that in His time He can lift you up. Be blessed young soldier.

THE RESPONSE

Describe a time when you got rejected._____

_____

_____

How did it feel?_____

_____

_____

What was your response?_____

_____

_____

Would you have responded differently knowing what you know now?__

_____

_____

Day 19: Patience

"Be still before the LORD and wait patiently for him; do not fret when people succeed in their ways, when they carry out their wicked schemes."
— Psalms 37:7 NIV

THE MESSAGE

My wife, Lori, waited five years before we met. She had hit rock bottom in her life and was desperate for a clean start. She moved back to Sacramento, where she was born, seeking a change of pace after losing her job as a head softball coach in college. Having been engaged once already, she had been close to getting married, but thankfully the wedding fell through. She knew in her spirit it wasn't the right thing to do, but the aftermath led her down a path that was hard and painful. A series of bad relationship decisions, losing her job, and life in frigid Lake Superior Michigan had spiraled her to a place she'd never been before. That's when a conversation with her dad changed everything.

71

He suggested that she move back to Sacramento to be with family. Even though her parents live in Oklahoma, the rest of her extended family live in California. Lori pondered the idea and ultimately decided that a change of scenery and warmer weather might do her some good. With the move, she also decided to give up seeking any kind of relationship except with her Creator. For five years she remained single and didn't date. Go back and read that last sentence again. *Five* years. She didn't pursue anyone or have a desire for a boyfriend for five years in her thirties! While all of her friends were getting married and starting a family, she became so content with her relationship with God that she didn't even want a guy. Incredible! During those five years of singleness, the Lord restored my wife. He built her back up, gave her the confidence that she had lost, the security that she'd been longing for, and the strength to be completely whole without depending on a man to satisfy her. As a result, she was as healthy and emotionally stable as she'd ever been in her life. Until she met me (ha ha).

There's an old saying that the best things in life are worth waiting for. It's hard for us as athletes because we want everything right now, but we don't realize that it's in the waiting where the Lord prepares us for our destination. It's in the waiting where He molds us, shapes us, and restores strength to our lives. Your teammates may be succeeding around you. Be patient. You may be second string, playing the role of cheerleader from the bench. Be patient. Allow the Lord to mold you during this time. Allow Him to prepare you for your moment so that when it's your time to shine you will be ready. Don't give up. For your breakthrough is right around the corner. Trust the Lord and ask Him to teach you, train you, and equip you in the waiting. Let me promise you something: you won't regret it.

THE RESPONSE

Have you ever had to wait to become a starter?_____

How did you process it? Deal with it?_____

_____

_____

Were you angry and frustrated or patiently waiting while supporting your teammates?

_____

_____

How did it feel to finally receive what you have waited so long for?_____

_____

_____

How long are you willing to wait for your breakthrough?_____

_____

_____

Day 20: Courage

"Have I not commanded you? Be strong and courageous. Do not be afraid; do not be discouraged, for the LORD your God will be with you wherever you go."

— Joshua 1:9 NIV

Kurt Angle is a two-time NCAA national wrestling champion. I'm not sure if you've spent any time around the sport of wrestling, but you will quickly learn that those guys are different breeds. They think different, act different, and move different. Sometimes I wonder what planet they came from.

Kurt was shooting for the Olympics in 1996 when he was thrown on his neck in the Olympic trials during the semifinal match. Somehow, he miraculously won the match despite having numbness in his arms and pain shooting through his neck. He went on to somehow win the

75

finals match and place for the Olympic Games in Atlanta the following year. After the match, Kurt went to get an MRI on his neck; the results were not in his favor. He had four broken vertebrae and two discs jamming into his spinal cord. The doctor said he had to shut it down or else risk permanent paralysis or severe issues for the rest of his life. The news crushed him. All his life he dreamed of being an Olympic gold medalist, and now he was faced with a decision that could have life altering consequences.

Kurt decided to get a second opinion. He went to another doctor, got another MRI, and basically got the same response as the first doctor. The only difference, however, was this new doctor offered a potential solution to help Kurt chase his dream. He asked Kurt how long he had before the Olympics. Kurt told him six weeks. The doctor said he wouldn't be able to train like normal because he would need to rest his neck. He would have to take twelve shots of Novocain five minutes before each match to numb his neck. About an hour after the match, he should expect excruciating pain from the beating his neck would take. The doctor believed that if Kurt was willing this was an option. Could you imagine? How much pain are you willing to endure in life to chase your dream? What are you willing to sacrifice? Kurt didn't hesitate. If there was a fighting chance, he was taking it. A doctor traveled with Kurt to the Olympic Games and was there to give him the shots before each match. Kurt won every match wrestling with a broken neck and took Gold in the 1996 Olympics in Atlanta Georgia. Talk about courage in the face of adversity. *Incredible.*

THE RESPONSE

How do you connect with Kurt's story?_____

_____

Would you take such a risk? What are you willing to endure to reach
your goals and dreams?

_____

_____

Describe a time when you showed courage in amidst adversity.

_____

_____

_____

At some point, we must trust the Word of God, and trust that He is with
us even when we can't see the outcome. Kurt didn't know the future. He
had to respond in faith that he was going to win Gold. True victory is in
the "letting go" of our fears and chasing down our prize.

Day 21: Development

THE WORD

"Let the wise listen and add to their learning, and let the discerning get guidance."

— Proverbs 1:5 NIV

THE MESSAGE

We all need to develop and grow. If you are the same man that you were last year, then you're not developing. Personal development begins with an understanding that you need more: more wisdom, more knowledge, more understanding, and more of God. The Bible says that the fear of the Lord is the beginning of all wisdom. The Bible is the first book I give young men in order to help them grow. It was the first book that challenged me as a twelve-year-old boy to think and act differently. The Bible is filled with wisdom beyond our years, and if we are willing to humble ourselves and open it up, we will begin to reap the benefits over time.

Not only do you need God's Word to help you develop, but you need mentors, coaches, and pastors as well. You need people who are going to offer you true guidance because they care about you, and not because they want something from you. Throughout my life I've been blessed with older, wiser, and more mature men of God who have helped me even when I didn't want it. It's not easy for men to seek out mentors because we think we can handle life on our own, but that's not the way Jesus lived His life. He chose twelve young men to follow Him. He invested over three years of His life into these twelve, and because of that investment we are here today.

Jesus' disciples carried His message till their death, in fact all of them were killed for their faith except the apostle John who died of natural causes. That's crazy. That's impact. That's life-on-life relationship, and if there's one thing I've learned in my thirty-seven years on this planet it's this: relationships are the most important commodity you have outside of time. Don't hesitate to pray for godly mentors in your life. Be on the lookout for peers and friends who have something that you don't yet have. Position yourself around those who you want to become like, because osmosis is a real thing. The more you're around someone, the more like them you become. It's no wonder ten out of the twelve disciples gave up their life for Jesus. They watched Him give up His life for them. *Powerful!*

THE RESPONSE

Make a list of your five closest friends. Describe their character qualities. What makes them special? What do they have that you want? Are they good influences on you? Do you sharpen one another and challenge each other to be great?_____

_____

_____

Do you have a mentor? Someone older to look to, ask questions and learn from? Write down two or three names of potential mentors you can start seeking out. You can never have enough godly wisdom around you._____

_____

_____

Are you a mentor to someone younger? Do you have anyone looking to you for wisdom, advice, and counsel?_____

_____

_____

The idea is to pass along what you learn to others. That way you continue to multiply God's kingdom here on earth. Let's get it!

Day 22: Faith

The Word

"And without faith it is impossible to please God, because anyone who comes to him must believe that he exists and that he rewards those who earnestly seek him."

— Hebrews 11:6 NIV

The Message

What I love about the Gospel (good news) of Christ is that it's so simple a child can understand it. That's fascinating. The Creator of the solar system, one of the most complex systems that man can study, makes the most important news ever known to mankind so simple that a child can understand it. That's incredible. Jesus said that faith as small as a mustard seed can move mountains. In other words, it doesn't take a lot of faith to believe. Have you ever seen a mustard seed before? It's about the size of this period. The mustard seed is one of the smallest seeds God ever created, but when planted, watered, and given sunlight, it becomes one of the largest garden plants in the world. Literally, from the smallest to one of the largest.

The fact that you are reading this devotional means that you are searching. You may be struggling in your faith right now, but you're on the right track. The Lord will reward you for earnestly seeking Him. He will not let you go if you diligently seek Him to fill your soul. Just give God what little faith you have right now, and watch over time as He increases, multiplies, and grows it into one of the largest garden plants in the world. Anything worth working for takes time to develop.

Tom Brady didn't become the greatest quarterback of all time by showing up and working just one day. It was a process that he committed himself too, and as a result, over time he developed into the GOAT. In order to get there though he had to put faith in the process. He trusted that what he was doing was leading him to the place he wanted to be. That's the same with you and your faith in Christ. You must commit yourself to studying the Bible, surrounding yourself with likeminded people who are on a similar journey, attending church, Bible studies, and praying so that your faith will begin to grow day by day. When you commit to the process, you will see results. It doesn't take a lot of faith. A mustard seed can do the impossible. Just believe.

THE RESPONSE

What letter grade (A–F) would you give your faith in God right now?
Why?_____

_____

What does "seeking God" look like to you?_____

_____

_____

Is it hard for you to believe in a God whom you can't see or touch?
Why?_____

_____

_____

Describe a time God showed up in your life in such a way that you knew
beyond any doubt that it was Him?_____

_____

_____

Day 23: Letdown

THE WORD

"For if you forgive other people when they sin against you, your heavenly Father will also forgive you. But if you do not forgive others their sins, your Father will not forgive your sins."

— Matthew 6:14--15 NIV

THE MESSAGE

Forgiveness is one of the hardest teachings of Jesus if you ask me. Have you ever been wronged before? Has anyone ever done something hurtful toward you? Have you ever been offended or lied to? Taken advantage of? There are three things that you absolutely will experience in life: 1. You will die. 2. Someone will let you down. 3. You will let someone else down. We live in a fallen, jacked up, messed up, sinful world, and you and I are contributors.

I got a phone call from one of my close friends. He's about ten years younger than me, but I consider him like a younger brother. We met at our neighborhood pool some years ago and bonded over our love of the Pittsburgh Steelers. He told me that his Venmo account got hacked and that he needed to send me three thousand dollars in multiple transactions to secure it. I would then Venmo him back the money, or do what I did, which was deposit the money into my bank account and get the cash out for him. I trusted him. I had no reason not to. He had never wronged me before. Even though it sounded suspicious, I trusted the guy.

After I gave him the money, I received four emails from Venmo the next day saying that the sender of the four transactions denied that he sent them and as a result my Venmo account was negative three grand. What! There must be some mistake. Surely my boy for over ten years wouldn't do that to me! I was hurt. After all that we had been through together, all he had to do was ask me if he needed money, but he probably didn't want to ask when he thought he could get away with this harmless transaction. Little did he know, I would be hit with the consequence. We have since worked it out through a few hard conversations, and he has begun the process of paying the money back and doing the right thing, but the reality still remains. No one is perfect; we all fall short.

Being let down in life is unavoidable, but how we respond is most important. Jesus teaches us to forgive those who wrong us just as our heavenly Father forgives us. How can I hold this experience over my friend's head when I mess up daily? Who am I to withhold forgiveness? I'm in the same boat as him and everyone else reading this today. In fact, the Bible teaches we are all sinners, and we have all fallen short (Romans 3:23). Jesus knew this, and His prayer on the cross while suffering immense pain proves His teaching to us. While hanging on the cross Jesus literally prayed, "Father, forgive them; for they know not what they do" (Luke 23:24 KJV). Wow. Even in Jesus' ultimate moment of betrayal and persecution for sins He never committed, He was practicing forgiveness. If Jesus can do it, then we can trust that through His strength we can do it to.

THE RESPONSE

Describe a time when you have been wronged. What happened? How did you feel? Have you been able to reconcile? Have you forgiven that person in your heart?_____

_____

_____

_____

Forgiveness doesn't happen overnight. It's a heart issue that must be dealt with daily. Just remember, forgiveness is not solely for the other person; it's also for you. When you *choose* to forgive you choose freedom.

Who has recently wronged you? Pray and ask God to give you compassion and a soft heart toward that person understanding that they need God just as much as you do. It's not easy trust me, but your freedom is worth it.

Day 24: Faker

"The LORD detests lying lips, but he delights in people who are trustworthy."
— Proverbs 12:22 NIV

THE MESSAGE

Have you ever been lied to before? I had a friend from college whom I recently reconnected with a few years ago. He began to tell me how life was booming, and how he was going to get me connected with all these professional football players to speak and share a message of truth with them. He was name dropping guys like Tyreek Hill, Stefan Diggs, Deebo Samuels, all big name stars in the league at the time. I knew my guy had spent a few years out of college with the Bengals, but I didn't know he was this connected to the NFL over ten years later.

Let's pause for a second. I have a dream of one day being a chaplain for an NFL organization. I live in Nashville, so being a part of the first team to bring a Super Bowl trophy to the city would be pretty sweet, but I'm not picky.

It was around March 2023 when I got a phone call from my friend excited about his cousin, DeMeco Ryans, getting the head coaching position for the Houston Texans. He proceeded to tell me he was going to be the assistant linebackers coach for the Texans. I was pumped. Immediately, I thought this was my ticket to pursuing my dream. Little did I know everything my boy was telling me was a lie. He was in fact cousins with Coach Ryans, but he never had an official coaching position, and after making two trips down to Houston with the expectation of meeting Coach Ryans myself, I realized that my guy was pump fakin' me. I have to admit, I tend to believe the best in people until I absolutely can't. Some say I'm gullible and green, which is true to an extent, but I just can't help giving people the benefit of the doubt as long as possible.

I couldn't deny his lies any longer after I had scheduled a trip for me and my son to go to a game in Houston. My friend told me he would take care of us and get us into the player family area after the game was over. Thank God I didn't tell my son; my plan was to surprise him. We were scheduled to fly out early Sunday morning before the noon kickoff. On Thursday of that week, he called to tell me that the Tampa Bay Buccaneers just signed him to be their linebackers coach. "If I'm lyin', I'm flyin'," he said. *What NFL team makes a coaching change like that in the middle of the season?* I thought. Not many, and if they do you will find it all over the internet. There was nothing.

That conversation was confirmation for me that I needed to step away from that connection. Sometimes, those who pretend to rock with you are only using you to boost their self-esteem because they know the truth. Or maybe they are just so blind to the truth that they actually believe some of the stuff they say. Either way, those are not the type of friends you need in your corner. I haven't talked to him since.

What's the lesson? Ask God to help you identify the faker, and steer clear from their influence. If you're like me, it will be difficult because you truly want to believe in people, but over time as you continue to put the fleece out and test the ground, God will give you clear eyes to see right through the lies. Then it's up to you to set healthy boundaries to protect yourself and loved ones.

THE RESPONSE

Have you ever had a friend like the one I just described? Do you currently have a friend right now who you have doubts about?

_____

_____

If you are not sure, ask yourself: Does your friend ever do anything for you? Do they ever encourage you? Do they ever pay for anything, or are you the one always picking up the bill? Do their stories match up? Do you have suspicions about their life? Trust your inner gut, the Holy Spirit in telling you the truth about your friend. If in fact you find out that they are fake, then it's time to cut ties and move on.

Another good way to test a faker from a real one is when you are at a low point in life. Does your friend try and encourage you or lift you up? Do you never hear from them unless it's about them and their life? That is a good indication where their heart is.

Above all, seek the Lord's wisdom and ask Him to show you the real truth about your friends. God will do it!

Day 25: The Eagle

THE WORD

"As iron sharpens iron, so one person sharpens another."

— Proverbs 27:17 NIV

THE MESSAGE

Who's your road dawg? Your home boy? The guy who's been there with you through thick and thin? Is he an eagle? Or a vulture? Does he soar to new heights and levels or seek to ride the backs of others and devour those beneath him? Does he work hard for his grades or cheat off others? Does he cut corners in practice or commit himself to getting better? How does he treat people with special needs? How does he treat his parents or girlfriend?

These are all questions that determine the character of your closest friends. This is important because who you surround yourself with will make or break you as a man. Your friends will elevate you or deflate you, so choosing them wisely is paramount. I've been blessed with many incredible friends over the years, going back to high school, but one friend I would like to highlight: Troy Smith.

Troy is one of the funniest guys I've ever met. For real. He doesn't even try to be funny; it's just a part of his God-given personality. I love me some T-Roy! We met through a mutual friend and had lunch at one of my favorite spots in town: First Watch. I was walking through a difficult season in my life, and I've never been shy to share what I'm going through, even if I've never met you before. Troy and I joke even today about that first meeting. He barely knew my name and here I was pouring my heart out to this guy. Unbelievable. It's amazing how the Lord works though.

Fast-forward almost six years later, and I know the Lord put Troy in my path for a reason. He's not only been a solid friend and mentor, but he's also a constant source of encouragement when I'm down or needing a fresh perspective on life. Troy is my guy. We share the same heart for the Lord and passion for influencing people. We both love the stage and the microphone. We push each other toward greatness. We challenge one another to be the best man that God has called us to be.

Sometimes it's hard to put into words how important a friend like Troy is. Simply put, it's someone who inspires you to be better in life. My wife makes jokes that she has to compete with Troy for my attention. Don't worry, though, I'm working on it. In all seriousness, however, pray that God would bring a Troy into your life. The type of guy who will sharpen you like iron, who will make you better, and in response you will do the same for them. Having true godly friends is one of the most underrated blessings a man can have. If you have one of those friends, let them know how much you value their presence and impact on your life. For if you want to reach the mountain top, you must fly with the eagles.

THE RESPONSE

Do you have "Eagle" like friends in your life? What's their name? What makes them special? _____

_____

_____

What do you admire about them? How do they sharpen you as a man? How do you sharpen them?_____

_____

_____

Do you have friends that are vultures? Do you need to cut ties with them? How do you know?

_____

_____

_____

If when around certain friends, you find yourself thinking and doing things that you know are wrong, it's probably a good indication that you should begin separating yourself from them. Remember: Bad company corrupts good character.

Prayerfully choose your friends. The trajectory of your life depends on them.

Day 26: Commitment

THE WORD

"Jesus replied, 'No one who puts a hand to the plow and looks back is fit for service in the kingdom of God.'"

— Luke 9:62 NIV

THE MESSAGE

Are you committed? Jesus was nearing the time for His death, and as He was walking one day, a few men approached Him saying that they would follow Him but first needed to handle personal business. One man needed to bury his father who had just passed, and the other wanted to tell his family goodbye before he left everything to follow Christ. Those seem like very reasonable excuses to delay following the Savior of the world, but Jesus is different. He demands our full and complete commitment above anyone and everything else, and if anyone has earned the right to place such a demand, it's Christ.

Who else in your life has suffered for you like Jesus has? Think about the person or persons who love you the most. Have they ever been tortured and crucified for you specifically? Have they ever had spikes driven through their hands and feet, beaten with a whip that rips the flesh off their body, and forced to carry a cross up a hill to hang on? Probably not. Jesus may sound harsh in our verse of the day when He tells these men that if they can't commit to following Him without looking behind them, then they aren't worthy to follow the King of kings. In actuality, however, Jesus has every right to make such a demand. He didn't have to come to earth to rescue us from sin and death. He chose to. He didn't have to come as a baby born of a virgin, completely humble and dependent on humans to care for Him, but He did. He didn't have to be born as a human and face temptation, sadness, grief, pain, and heartache, but He did. Jesus has every right to make the rules for the game, and if He says He must be number one above anyone and everything else, then He must be number one.

I wonder sometimes how I would respond if I were one of the men Jesus was addressing that day. Would I drop everything right there and follow Him? I don't know. What I do know is that Jesus completely changed my life when I was twelve, and I've never been the same since. I definitely haven't been perfect, and I still have my share of struggles with putting false idols in front of my Savior, but I'm daily trying to surrender and commit to serving the One who gave up *everything* for me. Are you committed?

THE RESPONSE

How did today's Word speak to you?_____

_____

_____

If Jesus were to ask you to follow Him like He did those men in Luke chapter 9, what *one* person or thing would cause you to hesitate?_____

_____

In your life, when have you been most committed to following Christ? What did it feel like?

_____

_____

Where is your commitment level right now?_____

_____

_____

How much energy do you put into your relationship with God? Is it the same effort you put into gaming? Working out? Your girlfriend? Social Media?_____

_____

_____

I encourage you to evaluate your commitment level to Christ and possibly put some boundaries around those things or relationships that get more of your commitment than He does. Trust me, it will be worth it.

Day 27: The Risk

"Now faith is confidence in what we hope for and assurance about what we do not see."

— Hebrews 11:1 NIV

THE MESSAGE

As you get older, there is more risk involved in your decisions because your decisions not only affect you but those closest to you. What's the riskiest decision you've had to make so far in life? For me, it was starting my own nonprofit organization. If you told me in my twenties that I would be the founding director and CEO of my own 501(c)3, I would have told you to find a therapist. I would've never seen myself starting anything from the ground up let alone my own organization.

Faith, however, changes the game for us as followers of Christ. Look at our word for the day. Faith gives us the confidence to make the jump out of the boat and walk toward Jesus. The apostle Peter and Jesus Christ are the only two people in history to have walked on water. If you know of someone else, please let your boy know. Think about it, you're literally walking on water like concrete toward Jesus. Peter took a risk when he hopped out of that boat and walked toward Jesus on the water, because last I checked water isn't solid (Matthew 14:22–33).

Peter took a risk. You and I must take risks in life as well. Peter didn't know the outcome of what was about to happen. We don't either. Fortunately, we don't have the luxury of knowing the future, which is good for us, because if we did know the future why would we need God? Why would we need to trust and depend on Him for wisdom and guidance? We wouldn't, and we would be more like robots than created beings with free will to choose. When I took the risk to leave a comfortable, good paying job with an organization that is known throughout the world to start my own organization from scratch not knowing the outcome, that was my "jump out of the boat" moment. Don't get me wrong, I did due diligence in praying and seeking the Lord with the decision while also consulting trusted mentors and financial donors who already supported my ministry.

I'll never forget one conversation in particular. I was talking with a trusted friend sharing with him about my indecisiveness in taking such a risk. He gave me some of the best advice anyone has ever given me. He said, "God is not the author of confusion, so you need to pray and ask the Lord to block this move if He doesn't want you to continue, but if He does want you to continue then ask Him to give you the green lights." That was the Lord speaking through him that day. That word was exactly what I needed to hear, and it might be the word that you need to hear today. By God's grace, we are four years into Frontline Ministries, and the number of lives that have been touched is overwhelming. If I wouldn't have made that jump four years ago it's sad to think where I would be now. I've always heard the greater the risk, the greater the reward. I can attest to the truth of that statement!

The Response

What risky decision do you face right now?_____

_____

No matter what decision you need to make use this process to help:

Pray: Ask the Lord for wisdom.

Talk to people that you admire and trust.

Move: Put faith into action and don't look back!

Many people in life fail to enjoy living because they are too afraid to jump out of the boat. Following Jesus is risky, but man is it rewarding. So jump!

Day 28: The Reward

The Word

""The kingdom of heaven is like a treasure hidden in a field. One day a man found the treasure, and then he hid it in the field again. He was so happy that he went and sold everything he owned to buy that field."

— Matthew 13:44 NCV

The Message

I'm a dream chaser, a visionary, someone who's always looking toward the future, for what's next. Being a visionary is needed and oftentimes people who are dreamers are high achievers and get things done. The problem is that when I get so focused on my goals and dreams, I forget the One who gave me those dreams in the first place. I begin worshiping the dream more than the dream giver. I forget that Jesus is my reward, not the sensation of accomplishing my dream. Without Christ I wouldn't have any dreams. I probably would have never moved out of my small hometown in East Tennessee. I would most likely have multiple kids by multiple women, and there's a chance I would be hooked on alcohol like my father. Jesus changed my life.

The Lord has been on me hard about fixing my mind on Him and allowing Him to be the One I chase and not the dream. I've noticed that when my thoughts, energy, heart, and focus is devoted to serving Christ, I have more contentment, peace, and satisfaction in life. I'm not trying to earn people's approval or gain people's praise. I'm just living life and enjoying the journey with whomever the Lord puts in my path that day. I'm still driven and competitive. I still want to accomplish my goals every year, but I can do so out of a healthy emotional state and not someone who's desperate.

The most content and satisfied times in my life are those times where I'm truly happy with Jesus and that's it. I'm truly at peace with the life He's given me, and like the old hymn says, "whatever my lot, He has taught me to say, it is well, it is well with my soul." Even if you accomplish what you set out to accomplish and you reach the peak of the mountain top, if you've done so in your own strength, you won't be fully satisfied. Just look at Coach Prime, Deion Sanders. He had it all: money, cars, houses, women, popularity, everything a man could want, but he still tried to kill himself. Why? Because he was missing the only One who could offer His soul true satisfaction: Jesus Christ.

When he surrendered to God and gave ownership of his life to Christ his entire world changed. For the first time in his life, he had a purpose that was greater than things money could buy. He was living for a Kingdom that will never pass away! Now Coach Prime is as driven as ever, not because of his own dreams, but because of God. The Lord is Coach Primes treasure, and that is enough for him. He can't lose now.

THE RESPONSE

Is Jesus your treasure? Is He the One thing you desire most out of everything in life?_____

What dream, goal, or vision do you sometimes want more than God?__

_____

_____

Could it be possible that in your seeking this particular goal, you have lost sight of what truly matters in life? How can you refocus? _____

_____

_____

Have you ever been so excited that you found something so valuable that you're willing to sell everything you have for it? That's the way we should feel about Christ. With Him, we have everything that we will ever need.

Jesus is the reward!

Day 29: Success Routine

THE WORD

"Do not merely listen to the word, and so deceive yourselves. Do what it says."
— James 1:22 NIV

THE MESSAGE

Every great athlete has a success routine. If you've never seen Steph Curry's pregame warmup, you need to stop reading this and go watch it. It's impressive. He does a series of dribbling exercises, game shots, and off-balance shots to prepare his mind and body for an NBA game. Then he always finishes with his signature shot from the tunnel and a hundred-yard sprint down the hallway into the locker room. Success routine. Steph has developed and tweaked the routine over the years, but it's meant to get him ready for battle on the court.

In Day 4 of this devotional, I shared with you my fitness journey of going 365 days without having a cheat day. No cookies, no cake, no Popeyes, no pizza, no mac and cheese, no chips, or fun for an entire year.

I'm sure you're asking, Why? I work with athletes for a living. It's what I do. In order for me to challenge a young man to take his game to the next level, I must be willing to do it myself, and for me, that meant doing something I've never done before in hopes to receive a result that I've never experienced before. Success routine. After I hit my 365 days without cheating, I thought maybe I would smash some Papa Johns to celebrate this accomplishment, but I've realized that once you do something every day for 365 days it just becomes a part of who you are.

You would think after such an accomplishment your boy would be looking like a miniature version of Dwayne "The Rock" Johnson, but instead I wasn't really impressed with the results. I knew something had to be off in my diet because my training has always been on point, so I did something that I never do. I took a picture of myself, circled the belly fat that I wanted to shred, and sent it to a friend from college who's a fitness trainer in Miami. It was humbling, but I needed help if I was going to breakthrough to the next level of fitness.

Thankfully, my guy immediately responded. He told me to give him two months, and he'll have me where I want to be. He put me on a macronutrient plan where I had to count how many grams of protein, carbohydrates, and fat that I consume in a day. At first it was tedious, and I have to admit I wondered what I had gotten myself into. He dropped my calorie intake to 1,700 calories a day, which is nothing compared to what I was eating, and my body was in complete shock. For two weeks I felt hungry all the time, like I was on a consistent fast, but what I didn't realize was that my body was in the process of making the necessary adjustments to the food I was giving it in order to turn back into a fat burning machine like it was in my twenties. I also realized that the reason I wasn't burning fat despite eating healthy was because I was eating way too much. My body couldn't burn the number of calories I was in taking, so I was stuck. You truly don't know what you don't know.

Fast-forward three months later, and I'm as ripped as I've ever been in my life. I feel great, and now what was once foreign and hard has become my new success routine. Every morning, I open my fitness app and log my food for the day. I like to plan what I eat, so I don't have to think about it. I can't always do that when I'm traveling, but if I'm home, that's my routine. It's becoming a part of who I am and what I do. It's my new daily habit. Now what about you?

THE RESPONSE

What is your success routine? What is something you do every day that helps you be successful as a student and an athlete?

_____

_____

_____

_____

What is one daily habit that you need to kill? Maybe something regarding your diet or wasted time on social media? Is it a porn addiction? Vaping? Smoking? What is it that's hindering you from maximizing your God given potential?_____

_____

_____

What is one habit you need to create? Something that will help you grow and not fall back. A Healthy habit that your mind, body, or spirit needs._____

_____

_____

Only you can **identify** and be honest about what you need in order to take the next step toward greatness. I'm gonna quote Nike here: "Just Do It." Don't be hearers of the Word only and deceive yourself, but *do* something. Take action! I promise you. You will not regret it a year from now.

Day 30: Levels

THE WORD

"Whoever can be trusted with very little can also be trusted with much,
and whoever is dishonest with very little will also be dishonest with much."

— Luke 16:10 NIV

THE MESSAGE

There's always another level. You may have dominated at the high school level, but can you dominate in college? You may have a successful college career, but can you succeed in the pros? I love Jesus' teaching out of Luke today. If God can trust us with the little He has given us, then He can trust us with more; however, if we can't prove faithful in the little, then why would He expand our territory or opportunity? It's the principle of faithfulness.

I'll never forget the first time I addressed a high school football team. I was a youth pastor at a church in a suburb of Nashville with a passion for athletics. It was a Thursday after their walk through in preparation for their first game of the season. I had the guys write down three personal and three team goals on index cards. We talked about the importance of vision as they began a new season. I remember standing on a cooler so I could see everyone. Afterward, the response I got from those young men changed my life direction. It was as if God Himself came down and said, "Matthew, this is why I put you on earth." I felt this overwhelming sense of belonging and purpose. I knew what I wanted to do with the rest of my life: sports ministry.

My journey began with one high school football team, and then I joined an organization called the Fellowship of Christian Athletes which allowed me to serve multiple high schools and multiple sports teams in our area. It was heaven on earth for me. When you can make a living and do what you're passionate about, you've made it in my humble opinion. I've been serving middle and high school teams for eight years, and now have an opportunity to work with a college football team.

It's been a dream of mine for years to get my hands dirty at the college level. My big dream is to serve an NFL team one day as their chaplain, but like our verse of the day reminds us, there's a process that we must go through in order for God to prepare us for our ultimate destiny. With every level I'm learning how programs work, how they are structured, what recruiting looks like, how to serve the various needs of college programs compared to high school programs. Every day is training for me, and I'm thankful for it.

Don't skip the process. You may be discouraged right now with the level you're at, and you may feel like you'll never progress, but stay faithful. The Lord is always doing more than you know, and the only way you'll never advance to the next level is if you quit. The time frame for advancement is up to God. We get impatient and want to level up immediately, but the Lord knows that there might be things we still need to learn. If He advanced us when we wanted, we would end up failing and falling flat because of character flaws that need to be dealt with. That's why seeking Jesus every day is so important. Finding contentment and satisfaction in Him is the ultimate goal. Then, just like the apostle Paul, no matter what situation we find ourselves in we can be content because we have everything we need in Christ. God has you currently right where He wants you. Embrace your now, because He's preparing you for your tomorrow.

THE RESPONSE

What's the next level for you?_____

_____

Do you ever feel like you're stuck at your current level? What is God trying to teach you right now at the level you're at?_____

_____

_____

Are you content with God? Or do you feel like you're always chasing the next level in life?

_____

_____

Are you maximizing all that God has given you today? How can you make the most of the opportunities He's already put in your hands?___

_____

_____

We must trust the process that God is putting us through in order to taste and see what He has in store for us later.

Conclusion

Well, how do you feel? What did you learn during this thirty-day journey? Did God speak to you? Did you connect with Him in a way that maybe you hadn't before? I pray that this devotional was a blessing to you and your walk with God, and I hope that you will use this devotional again or give it away to a teammate who may need some encouragement. You may be asking Where do I go from here?

You should find a Bible in a version that is easy for you to read and understand like the New International Version (NIV), New Century Version (NCV), or New American Standard Bible (NASB). You can download a Bible app for your phone, such as YouVersion or Bible Gateway. Begin reading in the book of Proverbs in the Old Testament if you want some practical, wise truth on how to live life and the book of Luke in the New Testament to begin learning about the life of Jesus: How He lived, thought, and treated others and about His birth, death, and resurrection. You can never go wrong learning more about your Savior. Whatever books you choose to read, make time throughout your week to read and study the Bible. By God's grace, I have been reading the Bible for roughly twenty-six years now, and there is no way I would be where I am in life today without the truth and guidance of

God's Word. There truly is *no substitute* for the Word of God. As I close, I want to remind you of who you are.

You are CHOSEN

You are GODS' SON

You are SPECIAL

You are UNIQUE

You are BOLD AND COURAGEOUS

You are HUMBLE AND KIND

You are SMART AND INTELLIGENT

You are GIFTED

You are TALENTED

There is no one that brings to the table what you bring.

You are divinely created and destined for greatness.

When the devil tries to lie to you and tell you what you aren't, go ahead and remind him of *who you are.*

Stay in the fight bro. For this world *needs* what you have.

Much love,

Coach Matt